THE INTERVIEW

(OR) THE TRANSPLANT VENOM CALLED CLAUSTROPHOBIA

by Chase Ramsey

EXIT PRESS

The Interview (or) The Transplant Venom called Claustrophobia

by Chase Ramsey
Copyright © 2015 by Chase Ramsey

Published by EXIT PRESS

The Interview was first presented by Warboy Theatre Projects at the EXIT Theatre, in San Francisco, on September 12, 2015.

Book design by Richard Livingston and C. White

For performance inquiries, contact Chase Ramsey (chasekeala@gmail.com)

For additional information about
EXIT PRESS, go to
www.exitpress.org

Paperback ISBN: 978-1-941704-08-0

EXIT PRESS
156 Eddy Street
San Francisco, CA 94102-2708
mail@theexit.org

First Edition: September 2015

Dedication

for Janessa Renee Ramsey

Introduction

"Absurdity" presents humanity stripped of the accidental circumstances of social position or historical context, confronted with basic choices. Martin Esslin

From the Greek dramas, the classical period, the morality plays of the Middle Ages, up to the late nineteenth century, elements of the Theatre of the Absurd have been found.

The term, "Theatre of the Absurd" was first coined by the critic Martin Esslin in his book titled, *Theatre of the Absurd*. It refers to a particular type of play that became most popular during the 1950's and 1960's. Absurd Theatre emerged during a moment of crisis in the literary and artistic movement of Modernism during the closing years of the 19th century, yet with economic and political upheaval during Hitler's reign up to Stalin's death, it almost disappeared. But with the rise in drugs, sexual revolution, anti-war protests, sit-ins, ban-the-bomb marches, Feminism, and Existentialism, the Theatre of the Absurd emerged with power. [Crabb]

World War II and the resulting Cold War age acted as the catalysts that breathed life in the Theatre of the Absurd. "The global nature of the conflict and the resulting trauma of living under the threat of nuclear annihilation put into stark perspective the essential precariousness of human life. Suddenly, one did not need to be an abstract thinker in order to be able to reflect upon absurdity: the experience of absurdity became part of the average person's daily existence." [Crabb]

Some elements of the Theatre of the Absurd:
• The experience of this world [of the absurd] is never debated, it is simply presented, shown in action;

• It satirizes a society that is petty and dishonest;

• It deliberately lacks any clear division between fantasy and fact;

• It constructs an environment which can depict/project mental conditions in the form of visual metaphors;

• It employs a precise use of language, constructed by a writer as their only defense against the chaos of the experience of living.

• It deliberately employs ambiguity as a device. What is reality, what is illusion... thus successfully destroying of our confidence in familiar things and places.

• It tends towards a radical devaluation of language, a poetry of images.

In Ramsey's play, *The Interview*, an interaction takes place between characters that mirrors the struggle of Sisyphus. Sisyphus was, according to Homer, a wise mortal who spurned the idea of death and mocked the Gods. As punishment, he spent a life in the Underworld, eternally forced to push a boulder up a hill. When the boulder reached the top, it rolled back down, and his task started again. Such as Sisyphus, the characters in the play are seemingly trapped in the menial tasks of business and struggle with the question of whether to remain or seek escape.

–Sherri Holcombe

References:
Crabb, Jerome. "Theatre of the Absurd" Sept. 3, 2006
http://www.theatredatabase.com//20th_century/theatre_of_the_absurd.html
"The Absurd and Beckett" http://wwwstaff.murdoch.edu.au/~serge/serge/Research.htm

The Interview (or) The Transplant Venom called Claustrophobia

By: Chase Ramsey

Better pass boldly into that other world, in the full glory of some passion, than fade and wither dismally with age.

–James Joyce

Premier Information

THE INTERVIEW was first presented by Warboy Theatre Projects at the Exit Theater, in San Francisco, on September 12, 2015. It was directed by Chase Ramsey; the scenery was designed by Chase Ramsey; Props by Sherri Holcombe; and the costumes were by Danielle Berry. The cast, in order of appearance, was as follows:

BUG ……….. James McKinney
MELROSE …… Jason Sullivan
MAN …........... Matthew Wade

Cast of Characters

BUG: A small man

MELROSE: A normal man

MAN: A superior man (doubles as a normal man)

Scene

A cold room. Simple. Dead. Familiar.

Time

Absolute.

Directors Note:

A solidus (/) refers to an overlap in dialog. Similarly, a dash (—) signifies an interruption or cutoff. The action and dialog should be played quickly and without forceful pandering. Avoid emphasis on the drama; allow the piece to speak for itself.

ACT I

Prelude (The Introduction)

It begins.

A dusty plastic tree droops in the corner of the room. Sad walls with rusted chairs leaning. The floor is covered in cigarettes and leftovers. We feel discomfort. It's familiar.

A man enters and we see streams of light fall on his dark and tired face. He smokes, obviously. That's most likely why he has a cane.

BUG In Greek mythology, Sisyphus the king was punished for what has been described as chronic deceitfulness. His punishment: to roll an immense boulder up a hill, only to watch it roll back down, repeating this action day after day … Forever …

A metaphor. A blockade. This tragedy we are about to unfold is about… Well, passion. Or, lack of passion …

(*beat*) I wonder if Sisyphus's shoes came untied?

Voices are heard in whisper. A violin plays.
We feel lonely. It's all confusing.
Voices are no longer heard.
It's familiar.

BUG (*Looking at the paper.*) Step One: The Interview

(*Looking out now.*) Melrose? Is there a Melrose.

A man steps forward and onto the stage. He is clumsy but we like him.

BUG begins to set up the chairs very slowly and carefully while MELROSE speaks. BUG is precise and accurate with the placement.

Part 1 (The Interview)

MELROSE I need a job. Isn't that obvious.

I can't seem to find my pen … It was a good pen, one with character. Smart. Stylized. I can feel a tantrum coming. A stress bubble … Right here in my chest.

Where does it come from I wonder? (*beat*) Nowhere I'm sure.

I'm missing many buttons. How can something hold without buttons. So it is with the dark.

When the time comes.

MELROSE Laughs.
He waits patiently experiencing nerves and ticks.

MELROSE Will they like me? Like yellow paint and gray skies?

A moment of nerves.

And I wait.

He discovers.

It is a test. I'm sure. My pen, where could it be … In a ditch, alone, hurt?
Well, it's a pen.

He sees BUG.

The surroundings are against me, I can see that …

He knows.

They … Took it. I believe they took it. A test. As I said before it is a test.
My first task is to seek the lost pen. I shall succeed as I need this spot
more than all others present. They need nothing. They need but a proper
place to feel stimulated … They need masturbation.

(*Beat*) Where is it?

MELROSE paces the floor, moving things. He looks in the most
peculiar of places and has no luck. BUG and MELROSE are
moving at a different pace from one another.

Trouble, that's what this place is. Full of trouble. (*beat*) I'm sure I like
trouble. If this is trouble then I'm sure I like it. Does it matter? Does it
matter if I like trouble? I will be trouble soon, I am certain of that.

A moment of thought.

The Plant. The Shrub. How could I forget nature. Although nature is
often forgotten by us common troublemakers. It … Must … Be …

MELROSE searches the plant and finds the Pen.

Yes. Here it is. The almighty Pen. The Pen, P.E.N. It is secured with me
as I have said it would be. I never lie and yet I will not discuss honesty
here. So the first test is a success. Should I stand and own it as if a mouse
sewing a wrinkled dress?

MELROSE approaches BUG.

MELROSE I have found it, I am ready for the next test …

BUG Please … sit.

MELROSE sits.

MELROSE Yes, are you …?

BUG The man.

MELROSE The man?

BUG Yes, the man.

MELROSE Do you …?

BUG Know who you are?

MELROSE Yes.

BUG No.

MELROSE That seems rude.

BUG It may. I mean nothing by it.

MELROSE Is this a place of trouble?

BUG That seems rude.

MELROSE It may. I mean nothing by it.

BUG I may speak candid but I don't know who you are. You could be a robber or a racist. We don't allow those here. Did you see the sign?

MELROSE I'm Melrose. I am related to your brother's wife.

BUG Oh, yes. How is she?

MELROSE Fine, I'm sure.

BUG Then you are?

MELROSE I am the alternative.

(*The cane*) Is that yours?

BUG It hasn't always been.

MELROSE So you're crippled?

BUG We are all crippled. It's these walls.

MELROSE Yes, I've been told that pink walls help for concentration. It must be hard to concentrate with … That.

BUG It looks better if you close your eyes.

MELROSE As does everything.

BUG So/ to the task.

MELROSE (*Excited now*) Will you ask me questions?/ I feel it is important that you ask me questions.

BUG Ah, yes the interview.

MELROSE Yes. The Interview.

BUG You would like to work.

MELROSE Yes, that's why I'm here.

BUG To kill yourself working?

MELROSE Or something. So … The Interview.

BUG Such a dead word now that I think of it. I'm sure it was created by an ancient civilization that felt proud with their buoyant creation. I think we should name it something simple.

MELROSE You have a lot of thought on the subject.

BUG Well, I should. It is what I have come to devour each day as I am pouring my soul into continuous and continuous motion.

MELROSE Like a teacher of Ballet playing Golf.

BUG The word interview is shit. We will now describe this experience we are about to have … Shit.

MELROSE I like it.

BUG Of course you do. Now, to the shit.

MELROSE *(A long pause, MELROSE is deep in thought. Or he isn't.)* Very Dangerous.

> *BUG clears his throat and fights through a moment of pain.*

BUG *(Looking on his clip board)* Yes … So …

MELROSE I'm—

BUG *(Reaching out his hand)* —No. Stop … Now, let's start.

> *Looks at the paper.*

Shake hands …

> *They shake hands.*

Sit down.

> *They sit down.*

BUG *(Reading directly from the clipboard)* What do you do? And where do you do it?

MELROSE This is a puzzling question. I don't often bill myself as a doer, although/ I like to do things when they should be done. Location is also puzzling because it is irrelevant to the activities in question. There is never a time I did something in a location I was specifically proud of and so discussing what I do and where I do it seems like an inappropriate question and I would answer it with a, NO. Thank you for asking.

BUG *(Nods his head in agreement)* Seems honest. *(Clipboard)* Has there ever been a time—

MELROSE —You have done this for many years you said.

BUG I will be asking the questions. That's what the paper says.

MELROSE Do you always do what the paper says?

BUG It says you get angry.

MELROSE Yes.

BUG Why would it say that.

MELROSE Because I get angry.

BUG Why?

MELROSE Outstanding question. Let me think … *(beat)* I get angry because of control.

BUG Ah yes.

MELROSE It's common isn't it?

BUG I'm not a doctor.

MELROSE Yes, but you have been angry.

BUG Once or twice.

MELROSE Have you counted?

BUG Four times.

MELROSE Then you are a master.

BUG I try to stay in control.

MELROSE Like a child on a bike.
You get to choose?

BUG I decide when the lights go on and when they go off.

MELROSE Is that your job?

BUG Depends—

MELROSE —Would that be my job?

BUG I ask the questions. It says that on the paper.

MELROSE Do you always do what the paper says?

BUG *(Intense)* Yes.

MELROSE *(beat)* Make it dark.

BUG Now?

MELROSE Yes.

BUG It would be painful.

MELROSE Confusing. It would be confusing.

BUG Confusion IS pain … Is this your anger?

MELROSE It's everyone's.

BUG Not mine.

MELROSE Are you sure? It must be.

BUG Not mine. I saw a young boy pull an arm off a kitten when I was eighteen./ Things were different then.

MELROSE (*To himself*) What did he say …? About …? The …?

BUG You're mumbling.

MELROSE Yes.

BUG What is it?

MELROSE Grey … Grey told me something important. We were in the grass sipping wine like two proud men who had passed the prime and settled in small breaths and cheap clothes. It was on a hill and under a tree.

BUG A hill? I don't know a Grey.

MELROSE He said to me … He said … "The only form of suffering is nonacceptance." He said that.

BUG So the darkness?

MELROSE Yes. If I turn off the lights it becomes dark?

BUG I assume.

MELROSE And the dark brings nonacceptance?

BUG Yes.

MELROSE And nonacceptance brings …

BUG AND MELROSE Suffering.

MELROSE Confusion.

BUG Fear.
It's a symbol I suppose.

MELROSE Of what?

BUG Of light and dark?

MELROSE What's your name?

BUG It's complicated.

MELROSE A symbol?

BUG Yes.

MELROSE Honest.

BUG Unfortunate.

MELROSE Proud.

BUG Not proud. This is work.

MELROSE Can you say it?

BUG If you don't corpse yourself.

MELROSE Laugh? I can't promise.
I'll get the lights.

BUG Would that make it easier?

MELROSE I don't know.

BUG Why must you do it?

MELROSE To remain in control

BUG That seems a contradiction.

MELROSE Contradiction? How funny.

BUG What?

MELROSE The word.

BUG Go ahead.

MELROSE You're ready?

BUG Never.

MELROSE Then let's remain.

   They sit.

MELROSE I found my pen earlier, as I had lost it.

BUG Another symbol?

MELROSE A test.

BUG Aren't they the same?

MELROSE Wait … The pen.

BUG And the paper.

MELROSE Let me try.

> *MELROSE leans forward and begins to scribble on the page with his pen disrupting and changing the rules. He then writes, in large letters "FREE."*

MELROSE You're free.

BUG *(He takes this in for a moment)* Free? No.

MELROSE Stop looking at the paper.

> *MELROSE runs to the light switch. BUG feels discomfort. He begins to cough.*
>
> *MELROSE flips the switch and the lights go out. BUG's cough begins to settle.*
>
> *A long beat ensues. After a moment we hear MELROSE speak.*

MELROSE How did I do?

BUG You should stay.

MELROSE And work here I suppose.

BUG Yes. You're hired.

MELROSE Thanks to the pen …

BUG *(beat)* And the walls.
My name … Bug.

MELROSE I understand that.

BUG Not funny?

MELROSE Very funny. You can't see me laughing because of the dark.

BUG Get the lights.

MELROSE Yes.

> *MELROSE flips the lights on.*

MELROSE Why are we here again?

BUG To work for an organization.

MELROSE Ah, yes. Waiting for death.

BUG It will come soon. I will show you how to work.

MELROSE Yes, show me.

BUG We should start.

MELROSE Yes, then we can end.

BUG Let me send the rest away.

> *BUG walks towards the audience and begins to shoo them away. He takes a few moments to try and get them to leave. BUG then turns back to MELROSE.*

They won't leave.

> *MELROSE walks and stands next to BUG, staring at the audience. They both try to shoo everyone out. They share a glance with each other. BUG clears his throat again and experiences a little more pain.*

MELROSE I suppose we should pretend they're not here.

BUG I suppose.

> *BUG grabs his briefcase. It is old, cheap and tattered. He takes a moment to adjust it so it is perfectly straight, settled on the chair.*

Part 2 (Work)

MELROSE To work then?

BUG A moment.

> *BUG, again moves the briefcase very slightly towards perfection.*

MELROSE To work then.

BUG Straight like a coffin.

MELROSE To work then?

BUG (*To himself*) Unrepresentable.

MELROSE Is that a word?

BUG Of course it is.

MELROSE In what dictionary?

BUG Well … There are many dictionaries explaining many different words. It's a word because I just uttered it. Does that not make it one?

MELROSE I suppose it does.

BUG Such it is with the dictionary.

MELROSE Roses.

BUG Meat.

MELROSE Dearth.

BUG Child.

MELROSE Bank.

BUG Dust.

MELROSE Poverty.

BUG Cancer.

MELROSE Nightmare.

BUG It's never what it seems.

> *BUG begins to adjust in frustration.*

MELROSE Does it matter?

BUG I remember someone telling me it does.

MELROSE Then it must.

> *An offer.*

Should I …?

BUG You shouldn't.

MELROSE I seem to /remember a …

BUG —I can get /it perfect …

MELROSE —A parable /of sorts …

BUG —Almost there …

MELROSE —About a blind /man seeking …

BUG —GOT IT. Perfect.
What?

MELROSE The parable.

BUG Yes?

MELROSE About the blind man who—

BUG —Yes, I know it.
(*beat*) Now, to open it.

MELROSE Allow me.

> *MELROSE opens it quickly, without a thought. He throws the lid back and gives a "tah-dah".*

BUG We will be fired for this.

> *BUG quickly, and gently closes the briefcase.*

I shall teach you.

MELROSE I will learn.

BUG Grasp the nose, pull gently up, release gently downward, then calm your hands ... Like so.

> *BUG begins to cough and breath heavily. He falls to the side of the chair and begins to gasp for air. MELROSE goes to his aid. It ceases and they return to business ... And so it goes.*

MELROSE (*In a gentle voice, like a child.*) Grasp the nose, pull gently up.

> *MELROSE gets nervous.*

BUG Release gently—

MELROSE —Release gently downward, then calm your hands.

> *BUG repeats "calm your hands" motion with MELROSE.*

BUG (*Still recovering*) Bravo, Melrose. This is very important.

MELROSE It does seem important doesn't it? I wonder which governing power released the responsibility to us. Could there be any other life?

BUG Only if there's another death.

MELROSE Oh. The Import.

BUG (*confused by his choice of word*) Important.

MELROSE (*Not quite correct*) Importance ...

BUG Yes. That's the one.
(*Beat*) Now, our J.O.B.

> *BUG carefully reaches into the briefcase and pulls out a paper kite and a marker. MELROSE is confused. MELROSE reaches in and pulls out the same.*

MELROSE (*Speculating*) A kite.

BUG Yes.

MELROSE A pen.

BUG Yes.

MELROSE I already have a pen.

BUG Not like this one.

> *MELROSE speculates.*

MELROSE (*beat*) Exactly like this one.

BUG Well … I don't make the rules here.

MELROSE Yes. (*beat*) But who does?

BUG Best we don't pry.

MELROSE It doesn't look like any boss types are about.

BUG Boss?

MELROSE You know … The one who provided the pen.

BUG I provided the Pen.

MELROSE No … The one who told you to provide it.

BUG Best we don't pry.

MELROSE I wonder where it lives … What it looks like …

BUG It is a man.

MELROSE How can you be sure?

BUG Because that's the way it goes.

MELROSE So it is … It's a confused business. It's just private parts … It seems too simple.

BUG We shouldn't have opinions.

MELROSE Well, that's your opinion.

BUG Round and Round it goes.

MELROSE Yes, silly business.

BUG To work then?

MELROSE For now.

BUG Forever!

MELROSE Forever?

BUG Like I said.

MELROSE That does seem like a long time … Forever.

BUG Yes … But it's who we are now.

MELROSE Our identities.

BUG So … The kite.

MELROSE This kite?

BUG It needs detail. Those deciding it is fit for play want to know fun resides. We provide stripes of joy to each part of this plan bringing it life and personality.

Then it sells. Tiz a very important job, yes, one of the most important jobs man attends to. Without us there is not life.

MELROSE Oh, very important.

BUG Let me teach you. And …

MELROSE Work.

BUG Work.

> *BUG chooses a corner of the kite and begins to slowly mark little lines almost like tally marks. After a moment he encourages MELROSE to join him. MELROSE begins.*
>
> *After a long moment of work.*

MELROSE (*Repeats in whisper*) Without us there is not life. No life … This work is very important.

> *After a few moments a man with a very sleek suit, clean shaven, and boss looking comes into the room. He is carrying a clipboard and briefcase. He stares for a moment, sets down his briefcase and starts to make his notes on the clipboard. MELROSE stares until BUG gets him back to work.*

MAN Tell me what you know.

BUG My Times Tables.

MAN Where does one begin and the other end?

BUG South America.

MAN How many languages?

BUG Three sir.

MAN A reminder that this is the most important job in the world and doing this job/ to your up-most ability will make you a very important person because this product can't be done without you here and you have been chosen to perform the most important work along with others that are the utmost people in this area although it is a small area and truthfully you're not extremely important but we think you're important enough.

BUG On my honor I will do my best to prepare this product in the most/ efficient and worthless way possible as I know it is the most important job in the world. I will live as though I am the walking dead being present without passion and courage giving up every hour for abuse and failure.

MELROSE I have been said to be the most efficient member of passionless product placers. I hate all of the great things that I get the opportunity to do. I love being a member of the most important nothing brand placing matter on devouring unhappy behaviors and sweat for a penny.

MAN (*To MELROSE*) You. What's today?

MELROSE Um … Wednesday.

BUG It is today, sir.

MAN Correct, no need to be specific.

MELROSE Yes, sir.

MAN No need to speak. Turn off your brain. Are you afraid?

MELROSE Yes.

MAN Are you afraid?

BUG Yes.

MAN And so it is.

MAN Can you recite the oath with me please?

> *The men are drones.*

ALL Business is made to be passionless, soul crushing, and maintains to be the most popular cause of death. If I die I owe nothing to business, but business owns everything of mine. Be afraid. Be very afraid.

MAN Paperwork, in my office, over there, tells me to speak gently in an encouraging way. It says to be honest in my compliments. So my honesty is this: You are not the boss and you are not free … That ends the compliment. Please get back to the most important thing and …

> *He looks at his clipboard; doesn't finish his thought. After some time the man picks up his briefcase takes a big deep breath and exits.*

> *BUG holds it in.*
> *Once the man is gone BUG coughs. It is painful.*
> *It ends.*

BUG That was him.

MELROSE You were right.

BUG Yes?

MELROSE It's a man.

BUG Yes.

MELROSE I aspire to that.

BUG Being a man?

MELROSE He has passed many tests.

BUG None to be proud of.

MELROSE I don't need to be proud.

BUG I can't argue that.
(*beat*) Many wish to be there.

MELROSE Yes?

BUG They never seem to grasp it. Some are made for kites.

MELROSE Are you made for kites?

BUG Happily, I am. Content. Scared. Content.

MELROSE It's either this or that.

BUG Always this or that.

MELROSE Are you scared of that?

BUG As I am scared of this.

MELROSE Like the dark.

BUG Ah. You made it a symbol.

MELROSE It is.

BUG Like the dark, yes.

MELROSE And yet … We live in both. The dark and the light. As it has always been.

BUG I don't think we were made for both.

MELROSE And here we are. A couple of perverts reaching for the stars.

BUG I never liked that saying.

MELROSE Have you been called pervert often?

BUG Yes. Isn't that obvious.

MELROSE Yes.

BUG The thing about the stars.

MELROSE They're far away?

BUG Who said?

MELROSE Someone famous.

BUG Then it must be true.

MELROSE Yes, it must. Why are we here again?

BUG Working until we die.

MELROSE When will death come?

BUG It already has.

MELROSE That's odd.

BUG It's honest. Back to work.

MELROSE (*Absolute*) It's all relevant.

> *MELROSE begins to whistle a tune. BUG begins to enjoy as though he has not heard music in a long while. BUG begins to smile and thoroughly enjoy himself. He laughs and bobs along as the two taste the flavor of camaraderie. BUG experiences a small cough. The moment passes.*

BUG The moment passes.

> *BUG walks over to the briefcase repeats the steps and pulls out two small stacks of paper and one marker. He brings them over to MELROSE.*
>
> *BUG begins to cough. It is painful.*
>
> *It ends.*

BUG This is the most important job you can do.

MELROSE Is it?

BUG Of course it is. Not to me, but to them.

> *BUG again begins to cough as before and falls to the ground searching for his shallow breath.*
>
> *MELROSE rushes to him. It begins to pass. They return to business … As it always is.*

BUG (*Ignoring the pain*) Write a name at the top.

MELROSE (*About the Marker*) We need two of these.

BUG Today we have this. There were cutbacks.

MELROSE But it's, you know … (Important)

BUG That's what they tell us.

> *A moment of thought.*

Start with a name.

MELROSE A name?

BUG (*Writing*) A name.

MELROSE Which did you choose?

BUG (*Reading*) Richard Column

MELROSE Do you know this man?

BUG Not so much.

MELROSE Was he in the war?

BUG Yes. Like the rest of us.

MELROSE He has good language?

BUG Very good language.

MELROSE I will write his name as well.

> *A moment passes.*

BUG Then we make two boxes.

MELROSE Show me.

BUG Four sides. A box.

MELROSE Very good. That's very good. You have done this before.

BUG Oh yes. Many times.

> *MELROSE draws his boxes.*

BUG Above one write the word YES.

MELROSE As in?

BUG As in: Yes, I shovel coal for cripples.

MELROSE Ah.

BUG The other write NO.

MELROSE Hmm.

BUG As in: No, it doesn't feel good.

MELROSE Ah. Finished.

BUG And it's over.

MELROSE Just like that?

BUG (*With GUSTO*) The most important.

MELROSE Will I ever see this product.

BUG Perhaps, if you are allowed to vote one day this will be your ballot. Choose carefully.

MELROSE Work.

BUG Work.

> *BUG puts the marker in his pocket.*

MELROSE Perhaps.

BUG And again.

MELROSE And again.

BUG And again.

MELROSE Until …

BUG Forever.

MELROSE Ah yes. This is the work you were talking about. The one that will kill us.

BUG Yes.

MELROSE I think I am catching on.

> *They sit for a moment.*

No more words? Now we are stuck.

BUG Like marriage.

MELROSE What makes you say that?

BUG I heard it said … From a man … Working by the sea. He wore a hat.

MELROSE A hat?

BUG Yes. A sea hat.

MELROSE Ah, yes.

BUG He was sitting eating a sandwich from his lunch canister.

MELROSE What kind?

BUG Hmm?

MELROSE Sandwich.

BUG Mustard and Ham.

MELROSE Perfect!

BUG After a moment he paused and stared out to sea as I have often done when drunk on the stuff. He said in a man's voice, "Marriage … I am surely stuck."

MELROSE I envy him.

BUG Marriage?

MELROSE Oh no … Lunch.

BUG (*Spells out*) S.T.U.C.K.

MELROSE It's business isn't it?

BUG Depends what you define as business …

MELROSE I have never researched it, although some say "business is life."

BUG Yes. I believe the opposite.

MELROSE Opposite of life?

BUG Yes.

MELROSE Death?

BUG Yes.

MELROSE You believe this to be—

BUG —Death. Yes.

MELROSE Surely this is a place of trouble. Why are we here?

BUG To work until death.

MELROSE Will it come to that?

BUG That's the purpose isn't it?

MELROSE I can't think of any other.

BUG (*Nervous*) I signed the paper. The paper told me to never speak of this. I signed it.

MELROSE To sign is—

BUG (*It's all clear now*)—It's Suicide …

MELROSE What?

BUG To tell truths. This work … Business … It's—

Something shifts as MELROSE has an idea. We begin to lightly hear sounds, voices, creeks. The lights begin to slowly dim around BUG and MELROSE. The sound will get louder as the intensity of the scene progresses. The lights dim as the intensity of the scene progresses. This happens until it no longer happens. Watch carefully.

The rhythm of the language happens like a train pulling from station beginning slow and picking up speed.

MELROSE —I have a solution to our being … Stuck. If I follow my heart through that door there into the next room with the man, in there where others place their faith and seem to explore—

BUG —Faith? No need to use profanity.

MELROSE (*Fixated, changing*) Yes … I will go into that door. I will make an attempt as I did earlier today … Or was it yesterday … When I was here searching for my pen and attempting to accomplish the test … I will go in there and search again, or surrender to whatever is needed. I think I feel a bit of energy.

BUG Careful now. They have pills for that.

MELROSE Pills, Pills for everything.

BUG And anything.

MELROSE Have you taken time/ to notice?

BUG I try not to.

MELROSE The patterns/ that exist.

BUG We have work to do.

MELROSE That door is/ a fossil.

BUG (*Referring to the Briefcase*) Pesticides, braces.

MELROSE Detailed and scaled like/ a tree trunk.

BUG Pennies, Perfume.

MELROSE This room feels darker, and/ that one light.

BUG No. The same. Bright/ as day.

MELROSE I think out is the way in.

BUG Contradictions./ Contradictions.

MELROSE On the way out … I should get the lights!

BUG What for?

MELROSE Protection.

BUG What about me?/ Me, me, me, me, me.

MELROSE I can't think of that now. Two is too many to keep your eye on at once.

BUG Aspirations seem to be changing you.

MELROSE Change … Yes. That's the word./ Change, always change.

BUG Aspirations.

MELROSE The door is where/ I make change.

BUG It comes at a price.

MELROSE Being stuck is the/ best possible thing.

BUG I can't help you in there.

MELROSE I will stand/ taller.

BUG Work to do …

MELROSE I will wear socks/ in there.

BUG You don't need socks.

MELROSE That room will be filled with a hundred pens.

BUG You only need one.

MELROSE And I will/ wear suits.

BUG I don't control/ anything.

MELROSE And suits.

BUG No.

MELROSE And suits.

BUG Please.

MELROSE (*Yells*) I WILL BE THE MAN!

BUG Melrose.

MELROSE I WILL BE HIM.

> *All sounds and intensity cease to a single light peering through a doorway. MELROSE walks toward the light. He is changed now. The boss.*

Part 3 (Fired)

BUG (*Whispers*) The boss.

> *MELROSE exits and it becomes light.*

I wasn't expecting that. Or … I was. Yes, we knew it all along I suppose. Contradictions, contradictions leaving each face to droop a little bit lower.

(*beat*) I'm tired. I'm sure these bulbs need a change, a proper recycled trade-in I suppose. When they flicker … I flicker. Now that made sense, the first sense I have heard since … Since …

(*beat*) I'm tired. It feels as though my pants are loose. Not much food today … What was it the philosopher said about a loose belt …

(*beat*) I am tired. Could use a cup of … What do they call the … The stuff to cure a tired morning … Or afternoon, I never really know. It doesn't need a name in order to work it's magic.

> *BUG stumbles to the briefcase and looks inside. He pulls out the kite and reaches into his pocket for the marker. As he pulls the marker out a piece of paper falls out with it. He unfolds the piece of paper to reveal there is nothing but a circle drawn in marker.*

BUG (*A memory*) This … this paper … from … from Bug. The Bug before me.

The shape. The shape he spoke of before. "A symbol" he said. Always a symbol.

> *BUG looks for a long moment. Then it's clear.*

Sisyphus … I understand. A circle. A boulder … The boss becomes the unemployed. The unemployed becomes the boss. I stay right where I was yesterday. Pushing … Uphill.

It is a circle, a hill. I understand business. I understand work. If work is death then death is freedom. Without passion we are oysters in a can waiting for …

> *It hurts now. BUG see's everything he has lost.*

BUG I'm sure Sisyphus saw the sunset from the top of that hill. Some of us only see

> *He knows.*

Walls.

> *Just then a MAN enters the space. He is very familiar, we have seen him before but with cleaner clothes and a straighter back.*

This MAN is a deformation of what we saw. No longer the boss but the unemployed.

On the contrary, BUG is reformed from what we knew of him. He is enlightened.

Translucent, sharp, recognizable … sonorous? I have doubts.

BUG waits. The MAN looks around. He enters the space.

BUG steps behind the shrub.

The MAN walks with dragging shoes and loud breath. He sits down in a chair. It repeats.

Part 4 (Meaning)

MAN I can't seem to find my pen … It was a good pen, one with character. Smart. Stylized. I can feel a tantrum coming. A stress bubble … Right here in my chest. Where does it come from I wonder. Nowhere I am sure. I'm—

BUG interrupts.

BUG I am the man.

MAN Yes, so am I.

BUG I will match your posture and we will start.

MAN So you know me?

BUG Yes, and you know me. From another life.

MAN Yes? It's a blur.

BUG Stay here with your ignorance awhile. I must prepare … Something.

(*Clearer now*) I must prepare something. You have big shoes to fill.

BUG prepares the space for another Interview. This time he does it in a sloppy manner.

MAN Shoes?

BUG Yes, I know it seems silly.

MAN But I'm here for—

BUG Yes, I know. To contradict. To poison. To dream.
(*A change*) To change. While the walls stay the same. I have been a wall for a very long time.

(A beat)

BUG Help yourself too … Uh … Sit down.

> *BUG begins to take off his shoes.*

Do you like symbols?

MAN Symbols? Yes. I think I do? Do you have a definition?

BUG No not today. Your name is—

MAN —Grey.

BUG No no, your name is bug now. Fair warning, this place will kill you.

MAN I'm not afraid of death.

BUG I'm sure … So we work here, or places like it somewhere out there.

MAN I don't think—

BUG —Don't think, yes very good.

> *BUG's shoes are now removed. He stands.*

Now Bug. Come sit here, on this piece of history.

MAN I'm here to—

BUG —Come sit, please.

> *The MAN trades chairs.*

Take off your shoes and slip into mine.

> *The MAN hesitates and proceeds. BUG dresses MAN.*

Here is your hat, cane, and most importantly … Do what the paper says it's important. Ah, yes. Your cigarettes to help you breath.

> *BUG breathes deep.*

This is a test. Stay here and see it through. I am sure you will know what to do.

> *BUG turns to leave and then turns back. BUG hands the MAN his paper with a circle on it.*

BUG This shape. A circle. It is a symbol. You will understand as you see the calluses on your hands don't belong to you. When you finally see the view at the top of the hill … (*beat*) You're on your way back down again. Careful now.

> *BUG exits.*

The MAN sits for a moment and then starts again.

MAN I …My first task is to seek the lost pen. I shall succeed as I need this spot more than all others present.

Coughing from offstage.

They need nothing. They need but a proper place to feel stimulated.

He contemplates.

MAN Step One: The—

BUG walks onstage in his underwear holding a large book. He walks to a corner of the stage and lounges, then begins reading.

MAN Excuse me … This is a place of work.

BUG puts his finger up gesturing MAN to give him a moment.

MAN I don't know what you mean.

BUG I've always wanted to read this … The man is waiting all that time for the fish, and the sharks take it for their own.

MAN This is a place of business.

BUG Oh, yes.

MAN What about your shoes?

BUG I don't need shoes.

MAN Are you sure?

BUG For the first time. I'm going to be a painter.

MAN But you will starve.

BUG Perhaps.

MAN I don't understand. How will you buy cigarettes?

BUG I don't know.

MAN I'm sure you're scared.

BUG Not today.

MAN You shouldn't say that.

BUG Okay. I'll be seeing you.

MAN Seeing?

BUG Or I won't. Remember that gift.

MAN (*Reaching for his pocket*) You mean-

BUG Yes, that gift.

>   *BUG approaches the audience.*

So, like Sysiphus the king we all have hands, and sometimes wear a crown.

But standing here at the top of the hill I'll never go back down.

Punch the clock, go on, It's fine, not many believe this man.

But I'll live in a box and paint what I see, because it's the only thing I can.

Just look at the walls.

>   *BUG touches the man's face and exits. We hear voices.*
>
>   *Comfortable now. Silence.*
>
>   *Purpose.*
>
>   *A deep breath.*
>
>   *The MAN is afraid. He does the only thing he knows how to do. He turns to us.*

Part 5 (A Circle)

MAN Step One: The Interview.

>   *Blackout. End of Play*

ABOUT THE PLAYWRIGHT

Chase Ramsey, Founder of Warboy Theatre Projects is an award-winning author and director. Wrote *& Juan*, which won awards at film festivals throughout the western United States. Recently wrote the book for *Peter Pan's Great Adventure*, a musical Theatre for Young Audiences piece. Other produced works include *Goodnight Monday* and *A Shared Life*. Past work has been seen with the Berkeley Rep. Selected to join the Kennedy Center MFA Playwrights Workshop in Washington D.C. Past work has been seen with Berkeley Rep., Guthrie, Campo Santo, The Cutting Ball Theater, Sundance, Hale Centre Theatre, Scera Cener for the Arts, Utah Valley University, the EXIT Theatre, and others. Chase is a member of the Stage Directors and Choreographers Society. Undergrad, Utah Valley University. Chase lives with his wife, Janessa, and son, Jude, in the west.

MORE PLAYS FROM EXIT PRESS

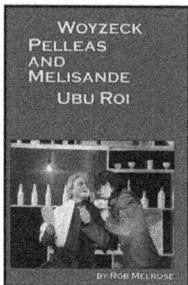

Woyzeck, Pelleas and Melisande, Ubu Roi: translated by Rob Melrose

"Rob Melrose is a kind of magician, and his theater, Cutting Ball, is one of the most exciting and integrity-filled enterprises going in the sometimes-shabby field of the American theater. These translations, lucid and sharp, are a beautiful testimony to the value of Rob's achievement." — Oskar Eustis

Three Plays by Mark Jackson

"Playwright/director Mark Jackson has made his name as a first-class theatrical provocateur. Gutsy showmanship, brainy literary instincts and laser-sharp satire mark his canon." — San Jose Mercury News This collection of plays by Mark Jackson includes three plays based on incredible historic events: *God's Plot*, *Mary Stuart*, and *Salomania*.

Songs of Hestia: Plays From the 2010 San Francisco Olympians Festival

Playwrights Nirmala Nataraj, Bennett Fisher, Stuart Eugene Bousel, Claire Rice, and Evelyn Jean Pine adapt some of Western culture's oldest stories, illuminating our present-day concerns with imagination, creativity, curiosity and passion.

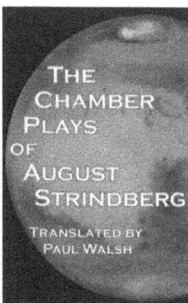

The Chamber Plays of August Strindberg translated by Paul Walsh

The Ghost Sonata, *The Pelican*, *The Black Glove*, *Storm*, and *Burned House*. Yale professor Paul Walsh provides modern translations while keeping Strindberg's "curiosity and his strangeness as specific and opaque as they are in the Swedish."

EXIT Press is the publishing division of EXIT Theatre, a San Francisco theater company founded in 1983. EXIT Press is distributed by Small Press Distribution of Berkeley, California. www.exitpress.org

.

www.ingramcontent.com/pod-product-compliance
Lightning Source LLC
Chambersburg PA
CBHW022349040426
42449CB00006B/797